THE RHODODENDRON FOREST

THE RHODODENDRON FOREST

with a translation of

The Legend of Alvargonzalez

by Antonio Machado

Denis Doyle

ISOBAR
PRESS

The Legend of Alvargonzalez was originally published in 1982 by North Light Press, Harrow; *The Rhododendron Forest* was first published in 1991 by Printed Matter Press, Tokyo, and Saru Press, Yokohama and Sedona, AZ.

This revised edition published in 2014 by

Isobar Press
Sakura 2-21-23-202
Setagaya-ku
Tokyo 156-0053
Japan

http://isobarpress.com

ISBN 978-4-907359-03-4

CONTENTS

I The Rhododendron Forest

Early Call 9
The Road from Fir Hill 10
Honesty Pennies 11
The Gorsefield 13
Lines 14
The Grasshopper Warbler 15
Border Country 16
Alfred Wallis Does His Spring-Cleaning 17
Peonies 18
Saecula Saeculorum 19
Lacuna 20
A Single Man 21
The Goose Gospel 22
A Trick of the Light 23
The Doctrine of Signatures 24
Last Job of the Day 26
After the Festival 27
Septuagesima Sunday 28
The Lark 29
Vera 30
Roadside 32
The Gardener 33
Dark Green 35
Leave to Go 36

II The Legend of Alvargonzalez
by Antonio Machado

Introduction 39

The Legend of Alvargonzalez 41
The Dream 43
That Evening 44
Other Days 46
Retribution 49
The Traveller 51
The Returned Emigrant 53
The House 54
Earth 57
The Murderers 59

The Legend of Alvargonzalez (Prose) 63

I

The Rhododendron Forest

Early Call

At six, fog erased the fields
And the cuckoo drew me up the lane.
The gate stood on the white banks of nothing
As the call wheeled outside our atmosphere.
I stood at the point where expeditions falter,
Numbed by the repeated statement I had failed to grasp.
The first and last thing in the field
Was a clump of white flowers, stitchwort.
I thought: that plant is a gatekeeper,
Yet I turned back.
But still I felt bound to pass on the coded message,
Pulling the receiver into the cottage garden
So that in London your drowsy ears
Would hear the cuckoo's call,
Still ringing unanswered at the edge of the world.

The Road from Fir Hill

The horned church at the end of the valley
Sends the sea wind up
In regular sweeps like bell strokes,
In white tongues of mist
Tolling a silent echo
Of curved water falling a mile away.
Two hedges, billowing brambles, draw together.
No car and no movement of mine
Disturbs the navigation of one stubborn bee,
Cutting three times across the wind
To the only bloom left
At the top of a foxglove, a bell set in a tower.
Beyond the valley, flooded
By a cloud that must have emptied the beaches,
Light pours on the sea
And the church above, making it small and browner.
The hare church at the end of the valley,
Guarding a field of its own flowers
Or a blue sea sounding its own bells.

Honesty Pennies

Seven years old and not in a state of grace,
I had stolen a handful of green stones from the graveyard
And, worse, I had gone with a girl of my own age
Out beyond the tombs where they filled the jars.
Our crime was to pick the pods of honesty
That hung on bony bushes near blackening nettles
And, playing priests, receive them as hosts in our mouths.
They were round and white and wrapped our tongues.
Mauve clouds curled like chrysanthemums;
There was a smell of decay, merely floral.
But fear sprang up like a dusk wind to break our communion.
A trinity of terrors: poison, the dark, mortal sin.
We ran to our own roads.
The weight of my transgression rattled in my pockets.

Seventeen, shriven but not calm,
Walking out of confession, watching my shoes.
Black and pointed, my calves still feeling the strain
Of kneeling with toes off the ground so as not to
scuff them.
My feet were together at the kerb, two glassy summits,
Mount Inattention, perhaps, or the Heights of Frivolity.
The priest was devout but he was not in my shoes.
Suddenly, there was a taxi I could see my face in
And, looking up to meet my own eyes, I met hers.
Though they were reddened and stared through pale
straws of hair,
I knew who she was. I knew she remembered our rites
And understood that whatever you see from the window
Of a gleaming taxi on the way to your father's funeral
Sinks itself into your mind: reflections on black.

Seven days older, that strip of hedge was my home.
I lay full length in hiding; she must come soon.
I had watched a day – his flowers were sick in the sunlight.
The pollen of nettles dusted the elegant black
Of the shirt, the jeans, the shoes I chose for our meeting.
To have worn dark glasses would have dulled recognition
But the honesty pods were there. I tried an experiment
And placed them over my eyes: modishly small white glasses.
They broke my vision a little less than a tear does.
I swept them off. The dream of the day had tired me.
I knew she would not come to kneel by the grave
And I could never emerge from the hedge to meet her
Or ever escape the steady play of two memories,
Reflecting each other, like barbers' mirrors or shoes.

The Gorsefield

This field of gorse is only green in June.
All through the leafless months it flowers in corners
Until in spring that yellow, fierce for a flower,
Breaks out of the whole acre like a juice.
And in a month the green pods will be black
And throw their seeds in the sun with a dry whisper
You strain to hear even in birdless August.
But June is silent now; the yellow-hammer,
Gorse-headed bird who nests among the spines,
Does not address the sun that shows through cloud,
A round of white with nothing yellow on it.
Identify this morning as a flower:
A white camellia, negative of a rose,
Quite free of colour, smell or juice or thorn.
Thorn – still one sense resists the vacuum.
If I could traverse all the cattle paths
Among the gorse with eyes closed and not touch
A single spine, the stillness would be perfect.
The maze would yield, the green square open inwards.

Lines

I shall be spending March at a high latitude,
In a city like St Petersburg or Aberdeen,
A schoolboy, crunching through stone squares,
Counting hexameters,
Far above the northern limits of the vine;
Ice and angles
In a city the Romans never reached.
Today I met a southern suggestion
In a girl's dark eyes,
And a fisherwoman with red hands like a fierce dawn
Told my lowered head
That the ice was breaking at the harbour mouth.
My spring began today and this makes me different.
I should keep it to myself – some people here would not approve –
Yet I want to announce my deviation.
The ice will not allow me to emerge from my greatcoat
But I think I will unbutton the epaulettes.
The equinox will be here before we see a flower,
Light will come off rationing
And the broad blank stone days will disturb me.
But just now I am happy
Though exiled by imaginary lines.
I shall construct a March poem calm as Latin,
Vine leaves appearing, a dance of young girls
And fig trees covered with white blossom –
I suppose they have white blossom.

The Grasshopper Warbler

I suppose this lane once twisted to avoid things,
But over the flailed hedge I can see no obstruction.
This gleaming tarmac brook might as well be culverted
And rule a line across the stark fields
Where even grass blades obey the farmer's geometry
As the wind combs them out.
And now the hedge rises and runs double;
Here is a ruined cottage or the stump of it,
A ground plan in cob, its corners seeming
To soften under drizzle even as I look.
But while the house meekly ploughs itself under,
The garden has made its own monument.
A long strip, so narrow
That the cottager could bestride his strawberries,
Has become a passage roofed with boughs.
Sallows spring from the stone hedges,
Meet and overlap, burying the earth.

A loud call from under them, a sudden rattle
Awakens guilt like an alarm clock.
A grasshopper warbler, holding out in the abandoned strip,
Still refusing to accept defeat
Generations after the marsh was annihilated.
That rattling cry cannot be love
For another bird under the boughs
And if it intends to contact other outposts,
For acres on either side there is no land untenanted.
I have heard the grasshopper warbler before, but never seen one.
If I came here with someone else, we could approach from either end
And drive it out of the leaves to get a look at it.
But, at the same time, I would like to imagine
That it has some way of evading us.

Border Country

The first of June,
Nettles tower.
Hedges smell hot;
I want to go
To the lee of the city,
The fold in the map,
The green canal
That cannot flow.
By the silent rail
On the tarred bank
Is a house, left empty
Long ago;
There are words on the walls,
Glass on the floor
Where I leave my bag.
If I stepped below
To the hedged plot
Drowned in weeds,
I could clear a space,
Use my hands for a hoe
And stand there
On grey soil,
The first of June,
Too late to sow,
And in that space
A bird's call
Would spread,
As bruised leaves throw
Hot musk
On the still air,
Long sounds,
Separate and slow.

Alfred Wallis Does His Spring Cleaning

The white sun moves on the rocks,
Passes into the old rocks,
Deep as a gull's reflection
Flying over wet sand.
April in St Ives
And the sun has a companion,
A small man in black, old and lively,
Hurrying like a cloud shadow over the headland,
Two tins of ship's paint hooked over each arm.
Under his Methodist shell,
A black which contains all colours,
The energy charging his body
Dances on his skin like fleas.
Can't stop, have to paint my home,
The town, hills, every one of those boats.
Not the sea; that isn't my home.
And it can't get me now.
Anyway, the sea has no colour;
I'll prove it to you.
Long ago, I caught the sea in a bottle.

Peonies

They were wild in Spain;
I saw their leaves in the mountains.
Even in our soft ground and gentler seasons
They push into the air, already in bud.
Their first leaves are brown hands shielding heads
Like orphans anticipating blows.

In Spain they said,
'You must see the gypsy dancer;
She's nineteen now and perfect,
But these people lead hard lives;
She won't last long.'

In hard red, the dancers form a line
And hold the perfect pose
Without needing to move,
Though the blue of old age
Has already entered the scarlet
And the white seed-pods show through like skulls.

Saecula Saeculorum

A boy on his sandy knees in a blank room
Presses his hands tight as unopened mussels.
Though the dusking sea moves in the window
It has become an illusion controlled by a switch
Like the toy storm in the lifeboat shed.
I climbed a cliff, I climbed steps to come here
And all the time I was moving out of my element.
My face is hot; my hands are too brown for this light.
I would like not to wash them, to let the salt on them crystallise
When I clamber red rocks to a still bay and lie
Between the bulk of the cliff and the pressure of light
To watch, under three fathoms of green,
The huge grey mullet move
With the world riding them,
Proceeding to their own conclusions,
Like the blind heavy movement of words in a winding prayer,
As it was in the beginning . . .

Lacuna

When the fields opened like a Book of Hours,
When April had just struck me on the shoulder
And thrown me blue favours to wear in my buttonhole,
When I set out to do battle with bullocks
Or scale the swaying citadels of crows,
I never saw you, a girl in the fields,
Singing an old song, conscious of my coming,
From a green turret at the edge of the wood.

I am the curator of my childhood;
Something in me keeps the glass case dusted
And turns over one of the pages every day,
But now, alone, admiring my Book of Hours,
I think, with sudden regret, you were not there.

Because I saw you cry like a child over nothing
And could not comfort you as a child would have done
I cannot calm myself with illuminations.
The desolate O of your mouth is a hole in the parchment,
A lacuna in the spring.

A Single Man

I seldom get up early to scrub sheets in the sink
And throw them over hoops of dead grass
To construct ragged sierras
In the blank garden I have always neglected.
Now, lying flat, one forearm across my eyes,
I cannot blame the sun for a morning's lapse
From the indolence I readily resume.
Last week, I saw the sun through dusty glass unmoved
And knew it was still winter.
But today the light infected me;
I was driven for a while, but it is over.
Now I can be impervious
To the thrust of green, the gathering of bird calls
And the flap of the sly wind animating the sheets.
One of them, already risen,
Stumbles into the bushes in a torn shroud
Like Lazarus recalled to be a beggar.
I can resist the urge to cut a pole for a clothes line.
I scrub sheets in the sink so rarely,
It might be better to plant a tree for it.
It is March; there is still plenty of time.
A black poplar – up in five years –
Or, better still, an aspen,
And then the wind could test my stillness all summer,
Make the white wink of its leaves
Suggest the purposeful run of the sea.
But I shall be under the branches, defeating all movement
By finding the one leaf like the one wave
That always seems to stare out at you;
Drawing your gaze, a ship suddenly trapped by green glass
With the wind filling its sails, its sheets, its shrouds.

The Goose Gospel

A monk who had learned how to whistle
Wrote at the door of his cell;
The curved letters wound in a helix
And his prayers were the sound of the shell,
But the margin he left on the missal
Was gilded with light. His work done,
He shifted his bones, future relics,
And wrote in vernacular, *Sun.*
The quill in his hand seemed to quiver
And pull with the will to migrate,
The letters were slanting, subversive,
Like geese making heaven a slate.

Sun swarms on the mountain / the river
Rolls stones by my cell, and the land
Is reviving / I cannot be cursive /
The long chain is loosed from my hand.

A Trick of the Light

A tunnel of light breaks the clouds,
Thrusting back the horizon,
And as the air opens,
A line of birds far off
Cross a corner of the sky
Like a faint brush-stroke
Delineating hills.
As a child I used birds to draw distance;
Grey wings repeated the letter 'r'
Across uncoloured skies,
And though I never draw now,
As if a trick of the light has reduced me,
I begin to search for a pencil.

The Doctrine of Signatures

It is time I returned from the sea
To the fields round the place of my birth
And I can only regret
That it will not now be as I planned it.
I will never go out in old trousers, striding the fields like a rook
With wads of leaves weighting my coat.
There will be no derelict cottage
Where I sit at the smothering fireplace,
Hands always busy with herbs.
A village sight, vague through brown windows,
Webbed with cracks from the stones of scared boys.
Today, by chance, I discovered that the fields
On which all this depended have gone.

Now I hear my feet crunch
On new gravel, by a new gate.
Aimless I stand. In the raw house,
The receiver is stealthily lifted
And they tick down the wire, three digits;
A live fence cuts me off from the past.

I shall tell my tale to the blue van:
'I believe in the Doctrine of Signatures.
I am here to gather foxgloves;
Their leaves are good for the heart,
As they're heart-shaped, you see,
And there was one clump in particular
That used to lean out of the hedge here.
Just here. Just after the war,
When I was a boy, and when this was a hedge,
And I know I have travelled the world
In the power of that memory.
Good for the heart.'

So I have dictated this letter
To say it will not be my fault
If, when they abandon politeness,
Try to order me down to their station,
I attack them with useless ferocity,
Like a dog guarding a grave.

Last Job of the Day

The sweep who dumped our soot
Beyond the bearded apple trees
Crouched to steal snowdrops.
The empty sack under his elbow,
Stiff and square with grime,
Hid the trembling fistful from the house
As he stepped to his van, smiling to himself.
He turned too quickly
And scored the soft ground,
But held up a large hand as he passed me,
White seamed with black, a palmistry diagram.
The headlights, suddenly switched on,
Pushed the first darkness up the lane.

After the Festival

All night weary slaves dismantled
The swaying ziggurats.
At dawn, my ears still soughed,
The white of the sky was broken with veins
And wine began to drum in my head.
Vans left the field, swinging in surly arcs
Round a girl in a long pink dress.
She lay on her back,
Her feet oddly vertical,
And the weight of her dark hair,
Swathes of it flattening hawkweeds,
Seemed to push her face into a vertical, too:
A white screen anything might cross,
A place hands ought to shield.
But her arms were set neatly in the grass
And her hands, half-cupped, were trapping runnels of dew
Along the lines of head and heart.

Septuagesima Sunday

On Septuagesima Sunday I re-arranged my room,
I turned the pictures to the wall and let the cold resume
Its interrupted tenancy. I starved the sense of sight,
Pulling the ragged curtains close to counterfeit the night.

The wind between the floorboards made discarded papers rise,
I lay in bed considering the loose lids of my eyes
Which let the world leak into me, corroding my intent
On Septuagesima Sunday in the season before Lent.

If you measured with a missal it was time to start again,
Create a void with Sunday, winter, darkness, London, rain;
Like the slip-road to a motorway, marooned upon a verge
I had no choice, I had to wait for something to emerge.

If darkness had a centre, I could come with pole and string
To tramp around the field of night in one unbroken ring
And either find the plover's nest and bring the world to stare
Or tell them all triumphantly that nothing had been there.

The curtain flapped like canvas; I was troubled by the fear
That I had set out once before but in some other year,
Yet my dreams were not dissuaded and my mind would not relent
On Septuagesima Sunday in the season before Lent.

The Lark

The song of a lark
Drills the pale rock of morning.
He stands high
Over soft strata of wind,
Proud to have driven
A straight shaft in one breath
Down to the green vein,
The thin green vein where –
But he has already forgotten this –
His flight began and will end.

Vera

The school marched to Mass and September was dense on my spirit
Like mist on a jersey sleeve. Bells, both holy and secular,
Had parcelled the Sunday; they herded us safe from distraction.
But through the thick hedge of responses, the humming of plainsong,
Reports would reach me, tales of another boy's August
To set my mind's hill-tops ablaze with pagan bonfires.

'And then, well, you know, we, you know –' 'Yes,' I said, but I didn't
Know how you knew a girl; that, too, was part of the Bible.
In a vineyard, perhaps, or at noon on the roof of the palace
But not in a Dutch barn, behind a cricket pavilion;
That was not in the books, and the girl – she was always the same one –
Never shy Mary, proud Caroline, wayward Rowena,
Her name would be Vera.

It was Vera who waved to the coach, who looked up when the gate slammed,
Always out in the lane with her friend who was younger and plainer,
Who left with her friend and came back alone later, but only
To find a lost charm from her bracelet, who said she must go now
But stayed, concerned with a curl or to hammer with pebbles
The heel she broke on the cliff. The tales, interlocking,
Were all of them true though, like the True Cross, all the pieces
Composed many stories the faith of a boy never questioned.

Stood up by Vera, I waited three years in the coffee-bar.
The froth on my cup held a heap of brown sugar suspended.
It was useless to stay; she had gone, changed her name. She
no longer
Tied back her hair with elastic that made her eyes widen.
And the church had gone too, as its bells could no longer
command me.
So Vera has stayed in the church, canonised in a window.
Her pink and her black and her peacock blue shine like
the Virgin.

Roadside

I wake in a field, my body twisted,
My stiff arm loaded with unshaken dew,
The morning or my vision misted;
Prone, I observe brown thistle stalks, then two
Detach themselves. A hare leaps from my view.

The Gardener

The old man tells me blood is good for roses;
His words go with the movement of my spade
And, turning earth a minute, I can see
The shadow cast by petals on a trellis.
Delicate rose that was too high for me,
I tried to pick you, straining with one arm;
Vigilant thorns repelled me and you swayed
Back with your branch – mine were the only losses.
I sucked a finger, you sustained no harm
And seemed more perfect slightly disarrayed;
Is this a way blood is good for roses?

Now I recall what this old man has seen:
He knew a country double-trenched by war
And from that ugly cultivation grew
Red flowers of red blood that were not roses –
Poppies to deaden what the hurt brain knew.
'We will remember,' every soldier swore.
The poppies said, 'Forget.' Years intervene,
Then towns were turned up by their children's forces
And rosebay blossomed where the fires had been;
Its willow-leaf reversed meant, 'Weep no more.'
What are these weeds if blood is good for roses?

I listen to a man whose words repeat
And cling to him like the soil he turns;
That slow accumulation of the years
Has built a garden wall which nothing crosses,
His mind outlives his memories and fears,
He keeps his territory and he learns
From the familiar things around his feet –
All other words rustle like hedgerow grasses.

Tonight, if his arthritic pain returns,
It may remind him bones are good, that peat
Enriches earth and blood is good for roses.

Dark Green

Colours I see in the dark
Swing past my eyes like clustering meteors
And I feel that a seasoned astronomer
Observes them as always.
Some colours he ignores:
There is no red in the dream world now poppies are rare.
But always he searches for green,
Dark green half-lost in darkness,
Growing out wider like mushroom rings in a meadow,
Spreading arms like the oaks above;
Rings like the craters storms make in young wheat,
Like cat's-paws, the wind's footprints on a freshening sea,
When the ripples open like corollas
And inner petals appear, storm-roses, sea-green roses,
Until the astronomer pillows his head on papers
And dreams that the forest which surrounds his tower
Is sending its bushes and brambles out into the fields,
Encroaching further and further
To extend the domain of sleep.

Leave to Go

I must have slept a season on this bench
And now the dew is warping my long bones.
Let me roll sideways till I stand upright;
The sly goat slips his chain – no need to wrench.
I am enfranchised by the pitch of light,
The sky is bloomed like berries, and although
My locked feet still tap fugues out of these stones,
This blue day is my letter – I can go.

II

The Legend of Alvargonzalez

Antonio Machado

Estepa is the Spanish name of a white flower, the cistus or rock-rose. In Soria, north of Madrid, the high plains where rock-roses bloom for miles, are also called 'estepas', the steppes of Spain, great tracts of uncultivated land in a region of pine forests, dry rocky mountains and wooded ravines which appears not to be European in its emptiness. This is the setting for *La Tierra de Alvargonzalez,* the story of a murder and its consequences.

Antonio Machado (1875-1939) lived in Soria for only five years, from 1907 to 1912, when he was in his thirties, but its landscape can be recognised in many of the poems he wrote later in his life. He expressed Soria's importance to him in one of his few autobiographical notes. 'I married there, my wife died there and her memory is always with me'.

Alvargonzalez was first written in prose as a 'legendary tale' and was published by a magazine in January 1912; an early version of the poem was printed in another magazine three months later. In the early summer of the same year, Machado's second book of poems, the famous *Campos de Castilla,* was published, with the final version of *La Tierra de Alvargonzalez* taking up one section of the volume. A few weeks later, in August, Leonor, Machado's wife, died of tuberculosis; during the months when Machado was working on *Alvargonzalez,* her impending death had been known to both of them.

Alvargonzalez is unique among Machado's works. Initially conceived as a prose story, it was transformed into poetry and twice rewritten in the course of a few months at a time of intense personal suffering. The narrative itself was simplified to an archetypal story of murder and retribution while the setting in which it takes place was developed and made to loom larger, absorbing the human events in the remoteness of an indifferent landscape. Machado appears to have searched for a way to reconcile feelings disarrayed by the harshness of fate with a wide-viewing composure, and this is attempted by the evocation of the dominant, immutable-seeming landscape of Castile which he loved.

I have translated the final version of the poem, as it appears in *Campos de Castilla*; the main addition to the earlier version is the brothers' ride through the forest which now forms most of the section 'Other Days'. A translation of the prose version is also included here following the poem. Machado's own journey to the source of the Duero with which the prose tale begins took place in the autumn of 1910; however, the legend was probably invented by him, as there is no evidence that it was told by shepherds or sung by blind men. But in passing from a tale to a ballad the story changed and developed, just as a legend does. A reading of the two versions will show how this happened.

The Legend of Alvargonzalez

Young Alvargonzalez
Owned land; in other countries,
They would say he made a good living;
In Spain, we call that a fortune.
He fell in love on a fair day
With a girl who came from Berlanga,
And made her his in marriage
The year that he first met her.
That was a splendid wedding,
As those who saw it remember,
And when the return celebrations
Were held in Alvar's village,
There was music of drums and bagpipes,
Flutes, guitars and fiddles.
They had Valencian fireworks
And all the dances of Aragon.

Alvargonzalez was happy
In the love of the earth he tended.
Soon he had three boy children
– Fine assets for a farmer.
When his sons grew up, he settled
That the first would work in the orchard,
The second care for the sheepfold
And the church would have the youngest.

Cain's blood still runs in the peasant.
Envy armed for battle
Around the hearth of the farmhouse.
The elder sons married;
Daughters-in-law brought discord
Before they brought grandchildren.

They look across death in the country
To see themselves inherit
And can take pleasure in nothing
As they brood upon the future.
The youngest son, preferring
Pretty girls to Latin,
Having no head for study,
One day hung up his cassock
And left for distant countries.
The mother cried; the father
Gave him his birthright and blessing.

And now Alvargonzalez
Was old; his brow was wrinkled.
On his chin, the blue stubble
Began to turn silver.
One day, in the autumn,
He left the house early,
Alone, without his greyhounds,
Who were eager to go hunting.
He wandered, sad and thoughtful,
Through the golden wood of poplars.
He walked a great distance
To a spring of clear water.
He lay down, spread his blanket
Across a stone beside him,
And fell asleep at the spring's edge
To the lullaby of the water.

The Dream

And then Alvargonzalez,
Like Jacob, saw a ladder
Which rose from earth to heaven
And heard a voice call him.
But the three fates were spinning
And among the threads they twisted,
Some white, some golden,
Was a lock of black wool.

Three young boys were playing
Round the door in the farmyard.
A black crow was hopping
Between the older brothers.
Their mother sewed as she watched them,
Smiling and singing a little.
She asked, *What are you doing?*
They stared and made no answer.
Boys, go up the mountain;
Come back before nightfall.
Bring an armful of brushwood
And make me a good fire.

The boys had stacked their bundles
Upon the hearth of the farmhouse.
The eldest tried to light it
But could not make it kindle.
The wood won't burn, father.
Perhaps these twigs are sodden.
His brother went to help him
And scattered bark and branches
Over the great oak-logs,
But the embers were soon extinguished.

Then the youngest came and started,
Beneath the black bell of the chimney,
A fire to light the whole house.

Alvargonzalez, lifting
His third son to embrace him,
Set the child on his lap, saying,
So these hands made the fire!
Although you are the youngest,
You are the one I love most.
The older boys retreated
Towards the dream's edges
And, as they fled, between them
An iron hatchet glimmered.

That Evening

The full moon was rising
Over barren country,
A great globe stained with purple.
The two older brothers
Were walking home in silence
And saw their father sleeping
By the spring of clear water.

Their father's face was twisted
By a frown between the eyebrows,
A heavy indentation,
Like wood scarred by a hatchet.
He dreamed that his sons were coming
And had raised their knives to kill him
But only woke to the knowledge
That what he dreamed had happened.

And so Alvargonzalez
Was killed by the edge of the water.
His chest and side were bleeding,
Stabbed in four places,
And his neck was struck by a hatchet.

The clear flowing water
Told of a crime in the country,
Even as the two murderers
Fled towards the beech-wood,
The black lake in the beech-wood,
Below the source of the Duero.
They took the body, leaving
A bloody trail behind them,
And at the lake, which is bottomless
And gives away no secrets,
They tied a stone to the body
And gave their father burial.

The blanket was found at the spring's edge
And a trail of bloodstains followed
The path that led to the beech-wood;
But no-one who lived in the village
Dared to approach that water.
Besides, it was useless to dredge it;
The lake had no bottom.
A pedlar who travelled that region
Was tried and condemned in Dauria
And died in the murderer's collar.

Several months later,
The mother died of sorrow.
They say that, when they found her,
She lay with her face hidden
Beneath her stiff fingers.

And now the two brothers
Possessed the folds and the orchard,
All the wheat-fields and rye-fields,
The rich grass in the meadows,
The hives in the old elm-tree
Whose trunk was split by lightning,
Two teams of oxen,
A thousand sheep and a bulldog.

Other Days

Now the thickets were in flower
And the plum-trees white with blossom.
The bees worked, pollen-gilded,
And against the high towers
Where nests crowned the churches,
The storks were thin as pothooks.
There was green on the elms at the roadside
And the poplar-trees by the rivers
That seek their father Duero.
The sky was blue; the mountains,
Now free of snow, were violet.
The land of Alvargonzalez
Overflowed with richness.
He gave the earth a lifetime
But he did not lie beneath it.

Sombre, spare and warlike,
That beautiful Spanish province,
Castile of the great rivers,
Encloses mountain-ranges
Between Soria and Burgos,

That stand like noble fortresses,
Or, sometimes, like huge helmets
With Urbión to plume them.

The sons rode mules together
Along the high path joining
Salduero to Covaleda,
Below the pines of Vinuesa.
They were going to buy cattle
And drive them back to the village.
Through the close-set pine-trees
They began a long day's journey.
They climbed above the Duero,
Leaving behind the village,
The stone bridge with arches
And the idle opulent mansion
Of emigrants who struck lucky.
The river slept in the valley.
There was only the clatter of horseshoes
Against the stones on the pathway.
On the other bank of the Duero
A voice sang, full of pity,
The land of Alvargonzalez
Overflows with richness.
He gave the earth a lifetime
But he does not lie beneath it.

At the highest point of the journey,
Where the pinewood starts to thicken,
The older man, who was leading,
Spurred on his mule and shouted,
Devil take this pathway!
More than two leagues of forest
We have to cross by nightfall.

Two peasants, accustomed
To rough, craggy country,
Feared a night in the mountains
Because of a day they remembered.
In the thickest part of the forest,
Once more they heard the singing:
The land of Alvargonzalez
Overflows with richness.
He gave the earth a lifetime
But he does not lie beneath it.

The road beyond Salduero
Follows the thread of the river.
On both its banks the pine-trees
Attain full height, concealing
The great rocks among them
To the point where the valley narrows.
Strong forest pine-trees
Whose branches spread enormously,
Whose naked roots clutch boulders.
The bark of some is unbroken,
Their needles a bluish colour.
These are young pines – the old ones
Are thick with leprous toadstools,
Mosses and grey lichens,
Gnawing at the branches.
They fill the whole horizon
And overflow the valley.

Said Juan, the elder brother,
If Blas Antonio's cattle
Graze on the slopes of the mountain,
We've a long ride before us.

The miles we've come already
We could miss when returning,
If we went by the lake, the short way,
Through the pass, down to Vinuesa.

Bad country and worse travelling!
I swear I've no desire
To go there. No, we'll finish
Our business in Covaleda,
Stay the night, leave at daybreak
And travel back to the village
By way of this valley, for sometimes
Short cuts turn out to be longer.
The brothers rode by the river
And saw the ancient forest
Seem to enlarge before them.
The rocky side of the mountain
Closed in their horizon.
The tumbling river-water
Seemed to be singing or saying,
The land of Alvargonzalez
Overflows with richness.
He gave the earth a lifetime
But he does not lie beneath it.

Retribution

Although Greed had a sheepfold,
Barns to put the corn in,
Bags for keeping money
And claws, it had no fingers
Or skill in cultivation,
And so that year's abundance
Gave way to a year of poverty.

The fields grew blood-red poppies;
The wheat and the oats were blighted;
Frost burned the orchard blossom.
The sheep fell ill, victims
Of some malevolent sorcery.
The two Alvargonzalez
Were cursed by God in their farming,
And one poor year was followed
By long years of trouble.

One night in the middle of winter,
The snowflakes whirled in a blizzard.
The brothers sat watching
A hearth of dying embers.
Both their minds were anchored
To the same recollection;
Both were staring fixedly
Into the fading ashes.
No wish to sleep, no firewood;
The long night grew colder.
One candle flame was smoking
Against the darkened whitewash.
The wind made it gutter
And shine a little redly
Round the heads of the two assassins.
The elder Alvargonzalez
Breathed heavily and hoarsely
And broke the silence, saying,
We did a bad thing, brother.
The wind shook the door on its hinges,
Made the shutter tremble
And blew up and down the chimney
With a loud and hollow roaring.
And then there came a silence;
At times the candle sputtered

In the frozen air around it.
The second said, *Brother,*
Forget the old man!

The Traveller

One night in the middle of winter,
A gale whipped the poplars.
Snow spread the earth with whiteness.
A man rode through the blizzard,
Half-blinded by the snowflakes,
His black coat wrapped around him.
He came through the village, searching
For the house, stopped at the gateway
And knocked without dismounting.

The brothers heard a knocking;
Hooves clattered on the cobbles.
Both looked up together,
Full of fear and amazement.
Who is it? Answer! they shouted.
Miguel, came the answer.
They knew the voice of the wanderer
Who left for distant countries.

The outside gate was opened;
A man came through on horseback.
He jumped down, white with snowflakes,
Silently wept for a moment
In the arms of both his brothers,
Gave his cloak and hat to one of them,
Handed the other the bridle
And went indoors, expecting
The warmth of a good fire.

The youngest of the brothers
Who went across the ocean,
Led by a boy's impulse,
Had returned, a rich emigrant.
The black suit he was wearing
Was made of the finest velvet
With a wide belt of leather
And a curling golden watch chain.
Tall and strong-looking,
With dark eyes full of sadness,
He had a brown complexion
And his tangled locks fell forward.
The man who had come knocking
Was the son of a simple farmer,
Whom fortune seemed to promise
Love, power and money.
Miguel was the most handsome
Of the three Alvargonzalez.
The face of the eldest brother
Was spoilt by the heavy eyebrows
That met beneath a low forehead
And the second had eyes that wandered,
Never still for a moment,
Cold, hard and inhuman.

The three men contemplated
The sad hearth in silence
And felt the cold increasing.
Brothers, have you no firewood?
Asked Miguel. *No, we have nothing,*
Replied the elder brother.
Then, as if by a miracle,
The heavy door of the farmhouse
With its double bar of iron
Opened; a man entered
With the face of their dead father,

His white hair shining
In a golden light around it.
He carried wood on his shoulder
And grasped an iron hatchet.

The Returned Emigrant

Miguel bought from his brothers
Some of those cursed acres;
He had come rich from America.
The land was bad, but money
Shines better for the using,
Better in poor men's fingers
Than put in a jar and buried.
Miguel began working,
Full of faith and tenacity;
Meanwhile, his elder brothers
Worked on their own portions.
And now the fruitful summer
Returned to Miguel's holding;
The tall ears were bursting
With yellow grains of wheat.
And now, from village to village,
The word went round of a miracle;
There must be a curse on the brothers.
Now the people sang a ballad
That told the tale of the murder.
Bad was the death they gave him,
Those bad sons who killed him
By the spring of clear water.
They threw their father's body
In the lake, black and fathomless.
He gave the earth a lifetime
But he does not lie beneath it.

Miguel, with two greyhounds,
Went out, armed with a rifle,
One calm evening,
Between the leafy poplars
As far as the blue of the mountains,
And heard a voice singing,
Earth could not give him burial.
Through the pines of Revinuesa
They took their father's body
To the black lake in the beech-wood.

The House

The house was old and weathered
With four narrow windows,
Set between two elm-trees,
A hundred yards from the village.
The elms, like giant sentinels,
Gave it shade in the summer
And dry leaves in the autumn.
This was a house for farmers,
Rich farmers, but still peasants.
The smoke-blackened fireplace
With the two stone seats that flanked it,
Was easily seen from the outside
If the door to the fields was open.
Two clay stewpots
Were set among the embers;
The food of two families
Bubbling away in the fireplace.
On the right, were the yard and the stable;
On the left, the fields and the beehives.
Behind, a worn staircase
Led to the sleeping-quarters,

Divided between two couples.
Neither of them had children
So the old home was half-empty.
In one part, which was sunny
With a wide view, was a table,
A great board of oak-wood,
With two chairs of leather.
On the wall hung an abacus
With great black counters
And two old spurs were rusting
Upon a wooden chest.
This part had been deserted
When Miguel went to live there.
From that room, his parents
Used to see in springtime
The orchard full of blossom,
And in May's blue weather,
At the time when roses open
And the thorn turns white with flowers,
The stork would teach its children
To use their slow wings in flying.
And all night in summer,
When the heat makes one restless,
They heard the nightingale singing.
And there Alvargonzalez,
Full of pride in his orchard
And love for his young family,
Dreamed dreams of glory.
When he saw the face of his first son
Smile in the arms of his mother,
Or the shining head of a baby
Whose greedy hands were reaching
For purple plums in the orchard
And ripe red cherries,
Or if the autumn evening

Was calm and good and golden,
He thought he had found it possible
To live in this world and be happy.
Now the people sang a ballad
Which went from village to village:
House of Alvargonzalez,
What bad days are coming;
House of the two assassins,
Let no-one call at your door.

One evening, in the autumn,
No nightingales were singing
In the golden wood of poplars.
The cicada was silent.
The last few swallows
Must migrate or perish.
Now the storks were leaving
Their nests of broom-branches
On spires and bell-towers.
The wind had swept the elm-leaves
Over the roof of the farmhouse.
The three round acacias
That grew in the church courtyard
Were green still; the horse-chestnuts,
Now and then, were dropping
Leaves and green hedgehogs.
The rose-tree had red roses
A second time. The meadows
Shone in the autumn sunlight.
In hollows, in declivities,
On banks and in clearings,
New green was growing
Where summer's heat had parched it.
Rocks and barren summits
Wore clouds, leaden, rounded.

Below the vast pinewood,
Among withered bushes
And bracken turning yellow,
The streams ran, rain-swollen,
Through deep ravines and valleys
To join their father Duero.
The ploughed earth showed its colours,
Grey as lead or blue and silver
With red stains like iron-rust,
Bathed in a light of violet.
Alvargonzalez' country,
Set in Spain's centre,
Poor sad country,
Whose soul was born of sadness.
Fields the wolf crosses
When he howls in clear moonlight
From wood to wood through scrubland,
Where the rocks are wind-rutted,
Where white bones glisten,
Picked clean by vultures;
Poor lonely wilderness
Without one inn or highway,
Poor maligned region,
Poor lands of my country!

Earth

One day in the autumn,
It was time to start the ploughing.
Juan and Miguel harnessed
The farm's two teams of oxen.
Martín stayed in the orchard
To hoe the weeds that grew there.

One day in the autumn
It was time to start the ploughing.
Juan's yoked oxen
Came on, moving slowly
Up a hill against the skyline.
Thistles, burdocks, caltrops,
Wild oats and darnel,
Filled the cursed acres,
Resisting hoe and sickle.
The curved oak struggled
As weeds drowned the ploughshare.
It seemed that when, almost breaking,
It dug itself a furrow,
The earth closed up behind it.
When a murderer does the ploughing,
He will find the labour heavy.
Each time be makes a furrow,
His face has another wrinkle.

Martín, still working,
Leant on his hoe a moment;
Cold sweat bathed his forehead.
The moon, stained with purple,
Shone behind the hedgerow.
Martín froze in horror;
The hoe was covered with blood.

The emigrant found prosperity
In the land which was his birthplace
And took as his wife a lady
Who was both rich and beautiful.
The land was his. The brothers
Sold it all to him; farmhouse
Pasture, plough-land, beehives.

The Murderers

Juan and Martín, the elder
Alvargonzalez brothers,
Went on a sad journey
At dawn, high up the Duero.
The star that brings the morning
Burned high in blue heaven
And a tint of rose coloured
The mist in the deep valleys.
Grey clouds where the Duero rises
Sat on the peak like a turban.
As they came to the spring, the brothers
Heard the clear water beginning
A tale of a thousand tellings,
A tale it would keep telling.
The stream ran through the country,
Monotonously saying,
I know of a crime, was it murder
To take a life by the water?
While the brothers passed it,
The clear stream was saying,
He lay by the edge of the water;
The old man was sleeping.

When they returned that evening
Juan said to his brother,
I saw, by the moon's light,
A miracle in the orchard.
Far off among the rose-trees,
I could see a man leaning
Towards the earth; below him
A silver sickle glittered.
Then he turned his face towards me
And made a few passes

Over all the garden,
Then bent once more with the sickle.
His hair was white in the moonlight,
A miracle in the orchard.

The brothers walked in silence
From the pass, one sad evening
Of November, cold and cloudy,
To the black lake in the beech-wood.

At dusk, a red sun filtered
Through the old beeches
And full grown pine-trees.
They had come to a place of forests
With jutting rocks among them.
Here were mouths yawning,
Monsters with claws stretching.
Here was a shapeless hunchback,
There, a grotesque belly.
Grim snouts of animals,
Fierce teeth showing,
Rocks and rocks and tree-trunks,
Trunks, branches and branches,
In the deepest part of the valley;
Night, fear and water.

They saw a wolf emerging,
His eyes like two firebrands.
Now night enclosed them;
Thick, rainy darkness.
The two brothers wanted
To return; the forest was howling;
A hundred eyes burned fiercely
Behind their backs in the forest.

They came, two assassins,
To the black lake in the beech-wood;
Translucent water, silent
As the great stone cliff behind it;
The nesting-place of vultures
Where even echo is sleeping.
Eagles fly down from the mountain
To drink this clear water.
The stag, the doe and the wild boar
Come and drink together.
Pure lake of silence,
Seeming almost eternal,
Still water, holding
The light of stars within it.
Father! the brothers shouted
And threw themselves in the water.
Father! called the echo,
Repeating among the rocks.

The Legend of Alvargonzalez

The Prose

One day at the beginning of October, I decided to go up to the source of the Duero. In Soria, I got on the Burgos stagecoach which was to take me as far as Cidones. I settled myself in the front, near the driver and between two other travellers. They were an emigrant who was returning from Mexico to his village deep in the pine forests, and an old peasant, who had come from Barcelona where he had sent two of his sons to Argentina. Wherever you go in the highlands of Castile, you will meet people who bring America into the conversation.

We took the broad Burgos highway, leaving on our left the Osma road, lined with poplars which autumn was beginning to turn yellow. Soria lay behind us, with its grey rocks and barren uplands. Soria, mystic and warlike, guarded the gates of Castile long ago, a barbican against those Moorish kingdoms where the Cid wandered in his banishment. The Duero makes a crossbow curve round Soria. We travelled from it like the arrow.

The emigrant was telling me about Vera Cruz but I was really listening to the peasant as he discussed a recent crime with the driver. In the pinewoods of Duruelo, the body of a young farm-girl had been found, stabbed many times and raped after her death. The peasant named a rich farmer of Valdeavellano, who was being held on suspicion in Soria, as the man who had certainly committed this terrible murder and was doubtful that justice would be done because the victim was poor. In small towns, the burning topics of conversation are sport and politics; in great cities, they are art and pornography – the leisure pursuits of shopkeepers – but in the country, the only subjects that arouse interest are the work on the land and crime.

Are you going far? I asked the peasant.

To Covaleda, he answered. *What about you?*

I'm going the same way. I mean to climb Urbion and I shall go up the Duero valley. On the way back, I'll go down to Vinuesa through the pass of Santa Ines.

Bad weather for going up Urbion. God help you if there's a storm in those mountains.

When we arrived at Cidones, the peasant and I got down from the coach, taking our leave of the emigrant, who was to continue his journey as far as San Leonardo. We started the ride down the horse-trail to Vinuesa.

Whenever I have any dealings with country-men, I think how much they know that we do not and how little of our knowledge is of any use to them.

The peasant rode behind me in silence. The man of that country, grave and taciturn, speaks only in response to questions and is brief in his answers. When the question is unnecessary, he hardly condescends to reply. He is expansive only when he mulls over familiar knowledge in needless detail or when he tells the stories of his region.

I looked round at the hamlet we were leaving behind us. The church with its high bell-tower crowned by a fine storks' nest overlooked a few wretched cob cottages. Set away from the main road, the house of a returned emigrant contrasted with the neglected buildings. It was like a modern worldly hotel with its garden bounded by wrought iron. In front of the village, a barren expanse of jagged rocks spread out, furrowed with rust-coloured crevices.

After riding for two hours, we reached La Muedra, a village which marks the halfway point between Cidones and Vinuesa, and almost at once we crossed the Duero on a wooden bridge.

By that path, the peasant told me, pointing to his right, *you can go to the Alvargonzalez land. No-one has a good word for those fields now but they were once the best in the district.*

Is Alvargonzalez the name of their owner? I asked him.

Alvargonzalez, he answered, *was a rich farmer but there is no-one of that family round here now. The village where he lived was also known by his name – Alvargonzalez – and the property round it was the land of Alvargonzalez. If we followed that track we would get there in less time than it takes to reach Vinuesa on this road. In winter, when hunger drives the wolves from the woods, they cross that village and you can hear them howl as they pass the old Alvargonzalez sheepfolds, ruined and empty now. When I was a boy, I heard a shepherd tell the story of Alvargonzalez and I know that it has been written down and sold as a pamphlet and that blind men sing it around Berlanga.*

I asked him to tell me the story and the peasant began:

When Alvargonzalez was a young man, he inherited a rich property from his parents. He had a house with an orchard and beehives, two meadows of fine grass, fields of corn and rye, a small wood of holm-oaks not far from the village, some teams of oxen for ploughing, a hundred sheep, a bulldog and a number of greyhounds for hunting.

He fell for a pretty girl from the Burgos region not far from Berlanga and married her within a year of their first meeting. Her name was Polonia, the eldest and most beautiful of the three daughters of farmers called Peribañez. They had been rich in other days but their wealth was much reduced.

Everyone has heard of the wedding in the bride's village and the return celebrations Alvargonzalez held in his own village. There were guitars, rebecs, flutes and drums, Aragon dancing and Valencian fireworks.

In all the country the Duero waters, from Urbion, where it is born, till it passes into the province of Burgos, they still speak of Alvargonzalez' wedding and recall the rejoicing of those days, because the people never forget glittering sights and fine music.

Alvargonzalez lived on, happy in the love of his wife and the prosperity of his land and livestock. He had three sons and when they were grown, he gave the first the orchard and the beehive to care for; the second, the animals, and the youngest was sent to study in Osma because his father had decided that he should become a priest.

Farming people have plenty of the blood of Cain in them. Envy waged war in the house of Alvargonzalez. The two elder sons married and the good father took on daughters-in-law who, before bringing him grandchildren, brought trouble. They were bad women and so envious that they thought of nothing but the inheritance which would be theirs on the death of Alvargonzalez and, through brooding over their hopes for the future, they did not enjoy what they had.

The youngest son, whom the parents placed in the seminary, preferred pretty girls to prayers and Latin. He hung up his cassock one day for the last time, intending to study no more. He declared that he wanted to set off for America and dreamed of travelling over many lands and oceans, of seeing the whole world. His mother cried for hours. Alvargonzalez sold the holm-oaks and gave the proceeds to his son as his inheritance. *Take your share, my son,* he said, *and may God go with you. Go ahead with your plan and remember that while your father lives you have food and a roof over your head in this house, but that when I die it will all belong to your brothers.*

Now Alvargonzalez had a lined forehead and the blue stubble on his chin was turning silver. His shoulders were still strong and his head erect; his hair had become white only on the temples.

One morning in the autumn, he went out from the house alone; he did not go, as he usually did, between his eager greyhounds with a rifle slung over his shoulder. He took nothing with him and gave no thought to hunting. He walked a long way under the yellow poplars on the riverbank. He crossed the wood of holm-oaks and, when he was tired, stopped beside a spring which an enormous elm-tree shaded.

He wiped the sweat from his forehead, took a few draughts of water and lay down on the ground.

And Alvargonzalez, all alone, spoke to God and said: *My Lord God who made the earth that I have worked with my hands, to whom I owe bread on my table and a wife in my bed and for whom the sons I fathered grew strong: Lord God, for whom my sheepfolds overflow with white merinos, the trees in my orchard load themselves with fruit and the bees have filled my hives with honey, remember, oh my God, that I know how much you have given me and I know that one day you will take it all from me.*

He was becoming sleepy as he spoke; the shade of the branches and the water which gushed over the stones seemed to tell him, *Sleep and find rest.*

And Alvargonzalez slept; but his spirit was not at rest, because of the dreams that trouble our sleep.

And Alvargonzalez dreamed that a voice spoke to him and he saw, like Jacob, a shining ladder which stretched from heaven to earth. Perhaps that was a shaft of sunlight filtered through the branches of the elm.

It is difficult to interpret dreams when they disturb the form of our thoughts by mixing them with memories and fears. Many believe they can predict what is to come by studying dreams. They are nearly always wrong, but sometimes they guess correctly. In the case of nightmares that weigh down the sleeper's heart, it is not hard to guess the meaning. These dreams are past memories which are woven and twisted by the slow trembling hand of an invisible being – Fear.

Alvargonzalez dreamed of his childhood. He saw the merry glow of the fire under the wide black bell of the hearth and around it his parents and his brothers and sisters. The knotted hands of the old man were held towards the yellow blaze. His mother passed the beads of a black rosary through her fingers. On the smoke-blackened wall hung the shining hatchet the old man used for chopping sticks from the oak branches.

Alvargonzalez dreamed on and now it was one of the finest days of his youth. A summer evening and a green meadow beyond the walls of an orchard. Sitting in the shade on the grass as the sun sank low and an orange light tinged the branches of the chestnut trees, Alvargonzalez lifted a leather gourd and red wine ran into his mouth, refreshing his dry throat. The Peribañez family was with him; the father and mother and their three beautiful daughters. From the orchard and the meadow there rose a harmony of gold and crystal, as though the stars were singing together on the earth before appearing one by one in the silent sky. Night came and beyond the dark pinewood the moon rose over the quiet country, trembling and golden, a full moon, a beautiful moon of love.

As if the fates who weave and spin our dreams had put a lock of black wool in their distaffs, Alvargonzalez' dream grew dark and a golden door opened to sadden the sleeper's heart. Beyond the door was a hollow space of shadows and in its depths, barely visible, was the hearth. There was no fire or firewood in it. The hatchet, polished till it shone, hung from a hook on the wall.

The dream shifted to broad daylight. Three boys were playing outside the door of the house. His wife watched them, sewing and smiling to herself now and then. Between the two older boys, a glossy black crow with a steely eye was hopping up and down. *What are you doing, boys?* she asked them. The children looked at one another and did not answer.

Go up the mountain, my sons, and before night falls bring me an armful of kindling wood.

The three boys set off. The youngest, who had dropped behind, looked round and his mother called him. The boy came back towards the house and his brothers kept on their way towards the holm-oak wood.

And once again there was the hearth, a fireless deserted hearth and on the wall hung the shining hatchet.

The older Alvargonzalez boys returned from the mountain

as evening came, loaded with firewood. Their mother lit the oil-lamp and the first son scattered wood-chips and rock-rose twigs over the oak-logs and tried to start a fire in the hearth. The kindling wood crackled but the logs had hardly begun to burn before it went out. No flame leapt on the Alvargonzalez hearth, shrine of their household. The axe on the wall shone in the lamplight and this time it seemed as though it dripped blood. *Father, the fire won't light. The wood is too wet.*

The second boy went to help and tried hard to make it burn. But the fire would not light up.

Then the smallest one threw on the fire a fistful of twigs from the hearth and a red flame lit the kitchen. The mother smiled and Alvargonzalez took the boy in his arms and sat him on his knee, to the right of the fire.

Although you were born last, you are the first in my heart and the best of the family because your hands set the fire ablaze.

His brothers, pale as death, moved away into the far corners of the dream. On the right of the elder boy shone the iron hatchet.

Alvargonzalez slept beside the spring as the first star of evening shone in the blue, and an enormous moon stained with purple rose over the drowsy land. The water which gushed over the stones seemed to tell an old sad story, the story of a country murder.

Alvargonzalez' sons were walking along in silence and saw their father asleep by the spring. Shadows, lengthened by the evening light, reached the sleeping man without extending as far as the murderers. Alvargonzalez' forehead was marked by a shadow between his eyebrows like the dent an axe leaves on the trunk of an oak-tree. He was dreaming that his sons came to kill him and when he opened his eyes he saw that what he had dreamed was the truth.

His sons killed the farmer by the side of the spring. A hatchet blow on the neck and four thrusts of a knife in his chest put an end to Alvargonzalez' dream. The hatchet he had inherited from his grandparents, which had cut so much wood for the hearth, split the strong neck which the years had not yet bent. The knife the good father used to cut the brown bread he handed to his children one by one at the table had burst the noblest heart in the country. For Alvargonzalez was a good man in his own house but he was also generous in his charity to the poor. There were many who would mourn him as a father, as they had called often at his house or at other times had seen him on their own thresholds.

The sons of Alvargonzalez did not realise what they had done. They dragged their dead father up a ravine where a river runs on its way to join the Duero. It is a shady valley thick with bracken under woods of beech and pine.

And they carried him to the black lake, which is bottomless, and threw him in with a stone tied to his feet. The lake is surrounded by a huge wall of grey rocks stained with green, where the eagles and vultures nest. In those days mountain people did not dare go near the lake even on fine days. Visitors like yourself who climb to such places have made them lose their fear.

The sons turned back through the valley between tall pines and aged beeches. They could not hear the water sound in the depths of the ravine. Two wolves who looked up to see them fled in terror. When they were about to cross the river, it changed course and they passed over its dry bed. They walked through the wood so as to go back to the village under cover of darkness, and the pines, the rocks and the ferns made a path for them wherever they went as though they fled from the murderers. Once again they passed beside the spring and the water, which was relating its old story, was silent as they passed and waited for them to go before it continued its tale.

And so the two bad sons inherited the property of the good farmer who, one autumn morning, went out from his house and did not return because he could not.

Later, his blanket was found near the spring and a trail of

blood through the ravine. No-one dared accuse the sons of the crime; peasants are much too afraid of those in power. No-one dared to drag the lake because that would have been useless. The lake never gives back what it swallows. A pedlar who used to travel about that region was arrested and hanged in Soria within two months. Alvargonzalez' sons had handed him over to justice and managed to have him condemned by using paid witnesses. Man's cruelty is as fathomless as the black lake. The mother died a few months later. Those who found her dead one morning said that her face was covered by her cold knotted hands.

The spring sun brightened the green fields and the storks brought out their young ones to fly in the blue sky of early May. Quails called in the green corn. The poplars that lined the roads and rivers were turning green and the plum-trees in the orchard were full of white flowers. The land of Alvargonzalez smiled at its new masters and promised to yield as much as it had given the old man.

It was a wonderful year in those fields. The sons began to feel the weight of their crime less heavy. Guilt gnaws at the wicked when they fear punishment, God's or man's; but if luck helps them and fear takes flight they eat their bread in happiness as if they were blessed.

Greed had claws to grab with but no hands for the plough. When the next summer came, the hungry soil seemed to frown at its owners. In the cornfields there were more poppies and wild grasses than golden grains. Late frosts had finished off the fruit crop while it was still in blossom. The sheep died in dozens because an old woman who was said to be a witch put spells on them. And, if one year was bad, another still worse followed it. Those fields were cursed and the Alvargonzalez fortune declined even as the quarrels between their wives increased. Each of the brothers had two children and no more because hatred had poisoned the milk of their mothers.

One winter night, both brothers and their wives sat round

a miserable fire, which was going out little by little. They had no firewood and could not go out to look for it at such a late hour. A freezing wind penetrated the cracks of the outer door and they could hear it howl in the chimney. Outside the snow whirled in a blizzard. They were all watching the fading embers in silence when there was a knock at the door. *Who can it be at this time of night?* said the elder brother. *You open the door.*

They all stayed still without daring to open it. Another knock sounded and a voice said, *Let me in, brothers.*

It's Miguel! Open the door for him.

When they opened the door, he came in, covered with snow and wrapped in a large cloak, Miguel, the youngest Alvargonzalez who had returned from America.

He embraced his brothers and sat down with them by the hearth. They all remained silent. Miguel's eyes were full of tears and no-one looked him in the eye. Miguel, who had left his boyhood home, had returned a rich man. He knew of his family's troubles but did not suspect his brothers. His manner was that of a gentleman.

His skin was burned rather dark and his face a little worn, for America always leaves its mark on a man, but youth sparkled in his large eyes. His dark-brown hair fell over his broad smooth forehead in thick curls.

He was the best looking of the three brothers. The face of the eldest was spoiled by the closeness of his bushy eyebrows and the second brother had the small eyes, restless and cowardly, of a shrewd, cruel man.

While Miguel remained silent and abstracted, the brothers glanced at his waistcoat, where a thick gold chain shone out.

The first brother broke the silence by asking, *Will you live with us?*

If you wish, Miguel answered. *My luggage will arrive tomorrow.*

Some rise in the world and some go down, the second brother said. *You come here with gold and we, as you see, haven't even got firewood to warm ourselves.*

The wind beat against the door and the outer gate. The cold was enough to freeze the bones.

Miguel was about to speak when there was another knock at the door. He looked at his brothers as if to ask them who it could be at that hour and saw that they were trembling with fear. There was another knock and Miguel opened the door.

Nothing but the hollow darkness could be seen and a gust of wind dashed snow in his face. Miguel saw no-one at the door but he could just see a figure moving away through the white flakes. When he went back to close the door again, he saw that there was a great pile of wood by the threshold. That night, a splendid fire burned on the Alvargonzalez hearth.

Miguel brought back a fortune from America, though not such a large one as his brothers' avarice imagined. He decided to acquire property in the village of his birth but, as he knew that all the land belonged to his brothers, he bought part of it, paying them much more than it had ever been worth. The agreement was made and Miguel began to work the cursed land.

Gold made the bad men's hearts merry again. They spent it carelessly on pleasure and vice and reduced what they had gained by so much that within a year they had to return to cultivating the land they had deserted. In the meantime, Miguel worked ceaselessly. He ploughed the earth, cleared it of weeds, sowed corn and rye, and while his brothers' fields seemed dry and impoverished, his own were filled with golden ears. His brothers saw it with hatred and envy. Miguel offered them the gold he still had in exchange for the cursed land.

All the Alvargonzalez land was now Miguel's and it returned to its fertility in the time of the old farmer. The elder brothers wasted their money in wild debauchery. Gambling and wine brought them to ruin once again. One night they were coming back drunk to their village, having spent the day eating and drinking at a village feast not far away. The first brother had a deep frown and a furious thought in his head.

How do you explain Miguel's luck? he said to his brother. *The earth fills with crops for him and won't give us as much as a piece of bread.*

Sorcery and the black arts of Satan, answered the second brother.

They passed near the orchard and happened to lean over the hedge. The trees were loaded with fruit and further off, among the rosebushes, they could make out the form of a man bent over the earth.

Look at him! said the first brother. *He even works by night.*

Hey, Miguel! they shouted to him.

But the man did not turn his head. He went on working close to the earth, cutting branches or pulling out weeds. The two astonished drunks blamed the wine which confused their brains for the circle of light which seemed to surround the gardener's form. Then the man stood up and advanced in their direction without looking at them, as if going to another part of the orchard where he could continue his work. He had the face of their dead father. Alvargonzalez had risen from the bottomless lake to work in Miguel's orchard.

Next day, both brothers only remembered drinking a lot of wine and seeing strange things as a result. And they went on wasting their money to the last coin. Miguel worked on his land and God made him a rich man.

The brothers once more felt the blood of Cain running through their hearts and the memory of their crime drove them to murder.

They determined to kill their brother and did it by drowning him in the mill pond. He was found one morning, floating in the water.

The criminals mourned his death with feigned tears to allay suspicions in the village, where they were disliked. There were plenty who accused them of the crime in a whisper, though none of them dared to give evidence to a judge.

And once again the land of Alvargonzalez returned to the murderers. The first year they had fine crops because they were harvesting Miguel's work; but in the second year the land became barren again.

One day, the elder brother was bent over the plough, which painfully opened a furrow in the earth. When he looked round, he saw that the earth closed itself up and the furrow disappeared.

His brother was digging in the orchard, where nothing flourished but weeds and he saw that blood spurted out from the earth. He leaned on the hoe and looked about the orchard and a cold sweat ran down his brow. Not long afterwards, the sons of Alvargonzalez silently made their way to the black lake.

At nightfall, they passed between the beeches and pines. Two wolves raised their heads, saw the two men and fled in terror.

Father! they shouted.

And when the echo began to repeat, *Father! Father! Father!* in the hollows of the rocks, the water of the bottomless lake had already received them.

www.ingramcontent.com/pod-product-compliance
Lightning Source LLC
LaVergne TN
LVHW050942080826
845145LV00004B/1372

* 9 7 8 4 9 0 7 3 5 9 0 3 4 *